FOR ALL INSTRUMENTS

EXPANSIONS

2nd Edition

A method for developing new material for improvisation

by
Gary Campbell

T0059237

ISBN 978-0-634-00005-8

Houston
PUBLISHING, INC.

EXCLUSIVELY DISTRIBUTED BY

HAL•LEONARD®
CORPORATION
7777 W. BLUEMOUND RD. P.O. BOX 13819 MILWAUKEE, WI 53213

Visit Hal Leonard Online at
www.halleonard.com

PURPOSE

The purpose of this book is to expand and explore the sounds that can be created from the basic scales and chords that have been used in jazz improvisation and composition for many decades.

The patterns included in this book are intended not only to expose your ear to different sounds from these scales and chords, but also to help you more fully understand the structures within them and how they interrelate. This knowledge heightens your insight into music in general and will greatly enhance your concepts as an improvisor.

It has been my experience that some of the things I have practiced have not gone directly into my playing vocabulary. Rather, they, and the theory they embody, show up in my compositions. These compositions then serve as tailor-made vehicles in which I can express what I've learned through my improvising.

This book is far from being all inclusive as there is essentially no end to the patterns that can be created. The book is intended to explore the materials that are being used more and more these days and to give you a start in understanding them. Once you grasp what is contained in this book you should be able to continue on your own, applying these principles to any material you may encounter.

You will undoubtedly come across parts of these patterns elsewhere (in etudes, scale studies books, etc.). When this occurs, take note of how they are used in comparision to how we use them here. You will experience an increasing ability to analyze and better understand all the different music you encounter.

TABLE OF CONTENTS

CHAPTER 1
HOW TO PRACTICE PATTERNS

Since one of the main goals of practicing patterns is to increase your playing facility and understanding of various scales, you must use a slow, relaxed method of practicing. Practice each pattern slowly enough that you can execute the entire pattern perfectly.

It is very important to <u>use a metronome</u>. As you practice, concentrate on making each note fall exactly where it belongs rythmically and in tune. If you feel a bit confused or tense, you are going too fast. You should feel relaxed, lucid, and in control as you practice. At first, don't be concerned with velocity. If any part of the pattern feels awkward on your instrument, repeat that part over and over. For instance, on the saxophone the extreme lower and upper registers are technically more difficult to play. Therefore, more practice time must be spent on these areas. It is important that you be able to play fluently throughout the range of your instrument, without interruption. Try to make each note respond clearly, with a full sound, and in time.

Once you have achieved all the above (within reason), gradually increase the velocity. As you do this be sure that you stay relaxed and in control. Don't be in a hurry!

In this book I have written each pattern in only one key. Be sure you practice each pattern in <u>all keys</u>. Also, do not write anything out unless it is absolutely necessary. If you understand what you are playing there should be no need for it to be read. See it in your "mind's eye". A notebook full of patterns written out in all keys won't do you any good when you are improvising.

BASIC ROUTINE

Here is my basic routine for determining whether or not you have basic command of a particular scale. I will write the routine in C Major only. You should be able to play all the scales mentioned in Chapter 2 in these forms. Do these forms on diatonic thirds, triads, and sevenths. Also do them with diatonic fourths and three note and four note chords structured on diatonic fourths. (This is dealt with in detail in *Patterns For Jazz* by Coker, Campbell, Casalles and Greene, as well as other books).

Shown here are diatonic triads in the key of **C Major**.

BASIC ORDER
Ascending

Descending

REVERSE ORDER
Ascending

Descending

ALTERNATING ORDER
Ascending

Descending

ALTERNATING ORDER #2
Ascending

Descending

Now for a very important point. We must vary the way the patterns fall rhythmically. Here is a simple device I use. When the pattern falls into a three-note grouping (triplets) such as diatonic triads, and I have mastered this grouping, I then practice the same diatonic triads grouped into fours (eighth notes).

EXAMPLE: C MAJOR DIATONIC TRIADS:
In Threes:

In Fours:

If the pattern falls into two or four note groups (such as diatonic 3rds or 7th chords), practice them in groups of three, or triplets.

EXAMPLE: C MAJOR DIATONIC SEVENTHS:
In Fours:

In Threes (Triplets):

Two note groups played as triplets

EXAMPLE: DIATONIC 3rds

As Triplets:

Here is a practice technique to help hear what a pattern sounds like when applied to chord changes. Hold the piano's sustaining pedal down and strike the various chords that relate to the patterns. As the chord rings, play the patterns. This is a good way to determine which applications you prefer. (This also helps string and wind players to play in tune.)

In summary, concentrate, relax, and be thorough. Don't waste your practice time.

CLARIFICATION OF TERMS

Generic thirds - either a Major third or a Minor third.

Diatonic thirds - within a given scale, the distance between every other scale step. I apply this term "diatonic 3rds" to both diatonic scales (Major, Minor) and non-diatonic scales (Augmented, Pentatonic, Six tone scales, etc.).

Diatonic fourths - within a given scale (diatonic or non-diatonic), the distance between every fourth scale step (skipping over two steps each time).

ABBREVIATIONS

Maj. = Major
Min. = Minor
Ø = Half Diminished or Minor 7 ♭5
△ = Major seventh
+5 = Augmented fifth
W.T. = Whole Tone

CHAPTER 2
SCALES

Because of the wealth of books on the market today that explain and illustrate how to use many of the more commonly used scales, I will hurry past them to get to a few more seldom discussed scales. The more common scales used in jazz and its related idioms are: Major, Harmonic Minor, Melodic Minor, Diminished, and Whole-Tone. Check yourself by practicing these scales using the Basic Routine. The use of these scales is well documented in **Patterns For Jazz**, in David Baker's many books, and in a wealth of others. Here I will discuss the Pentatonic ♭3 scale, Pentatonic ♭6, Augmented scale, and Tri-tone scale. (Other scales formed by the combination of two triads will be introduced in Chapter 3.)

Note: Throughout this book you will see chords and scales that may or may not fit into the conventional system of key signatures (♯'s or ♭'s). The usual key signatures apply to conventional Major and Minor keys. In the case of scales or chord patterns that are in no key as such, they may be notated with enharmonic spelling (E♭/D♯, B♭/A♯, etc.). Flats and sharps may be used in the same chord or scale. This is done for visual ease.

IMPORTANT NOTE:

In this and other chapters, when chords are listed for application to a particular scale, the scale tone from which each chord is rooted will be indicated in parenthesis. If the root of the chord is not a scale tone, its distance from the scale root will nonetheless be indicated with a generic scale step number. Also, refer to "General Chord/Scale Cross Reference Chart" on page 46.

PENTATONIC ♭3

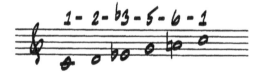

Best Applications: C Minor (1)
Sus 11, ♭2 (2nd)*
E♭ Major 7♯11 (♭3)
F 7 sus 4 (Perfect 4th)
A Half-Diminished (6th)
B7 ♭9 ♯9 ♯5 (Major 7th)

It can be used in places where the Melodic Minor would be used. In fact, it is a Melodic Minor scale, with the 4th and 7th degrees removed. I like to use this scale in diatonic thirds, triads, and four note chords built on diatonic thirds. See Chapter 6 "Diatonic Intervals and Chords From Scales Containing Fewer than 7 Tones". The diatonic thirds and chords based on the Pentatonic ♭3 scale are interesting because of the varying generic intervals the diatonic thirds form. They are:

MINOR 3RD   PERFECT 4TH   TRITONE   PERFECT 4TH   PERFECT 4TH

This succession of intervals sounds great when run through the Basic Routine for scale practice, page 4.

See Important Note

My favorite uses of the Pentatonic ♭3 scale are:

• sus 11, ♭2 (Phrygian), starting on the 2nd degree (i.e.) C Pentatonic ♭3 for D Sus 11, ♭2

• dom. 7th sus 4, a perfect 4th above the root, though this pitch is not in the scale (i.e.) C Pentatonic ♭3 for F7 sus 11

• dom. 7th ♯9, 1/2 step below the Pentatonic ♭3 scale's root (i.e.) C Pentatonic ♭3 for B7 ♯9 (altered)

I prefer this scale to the Melodic Minor scale because it gets a leaner sound. Played stepwise, it sounds more melodic, and less conjunct, with more variety in intervals.

To me the pentatonic ♭3 is more stable or static than the melodic minor. I believe this is because the pentatonic ♭3 does not contain the 4th and 7th degrees of its corresponding Melodic Minor. These 4th and 7th degrees form the tritone (7th and 3rd degrees) of the Melodic Minor's dominant, or a V7 chord. (i.e. in the C Melodic Minor scale the 4th and 7th, or F and B, form the 7th and 3rd degree respectively of G7, the scale's dominant.) When the Pentatonic ♭3 scale is played there is no implication of dominant or V7 function. In other words, there are no leading tones (4 to 3 and 7 to 8) in the Pentatonic ♭3. Likewise, all of this applies to the Major Pentatonic (1-2-3-5-6), giving it a more static sound than its corresponding Major scale.

PENTATONIC ♭6

Another mutation of the Melodic Minor scale can be found by removing the scale's root and 4th degrees. For example, from C Melodic Minor, remove C and F leaving D, E♭, G, A, and B. For our purposes we will invert this scale (D, E♭, G, A, B,) to G, A, B, D, and E♭. Consider the root to be G and call this G Pentatonic ♭6.

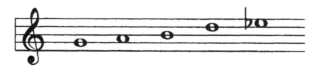

The main thing that distinguishes this scale from the Pentatonic ♭3 is its Augmented fifth aspect. Voiced from G (root position) you can get G+5. Voiced from E♭ you can get E♭ Maj.7♯5. The Pentatonic ♭6 Scale can function the same way as its related Melodic Minor and Pentatonic ♭3 Scales (a Perfect 4th higher) i.e. G Pentatonic ♭6 = C Melodic Minor, and C Pentatonic ♭3.

Accordingly, some applications for G Pentatonic ♭6 are:

> E♭ △ ♯5 (Aug 5th)[1]
>
> C Minor △ (Perfect 4th)
>
> G7+5 (1st)
> B7♯5♯9 (Major 3rd)
> F7♯11 (♭7)
> A ∅ (2nd)
> D 7 sus 11, ♭2 (5th)

Note: Try applying all of the preceding mutations to the Harmonic Minor scale (Removal of the 4th and 7th degrees, or the root and 4th degrees.)

AUGMENTED SCALE

This is a symmetrical scale with the scheme of 1/2 step-augmented 2nd, 1/2 step-augmented 2nd etc. It can be broken down in different ways. One way is to consider it as two augmented triads, a half step apart.
EXAMPLE: B+5/C+5

Another way to break it down is; three major triads, a major 3rd apart.
CMaj., EMaj., A♭Maj.

Note that the minor 3rd of each triad is also in this scale.

Some of its best applications are:
EXAMPLE: B+5/C+5

   C Maj7 (♭2,1/2 step)
   C Maj7 ♯ 5 (♭2)
   D7 sus or C Maj, E Maj, A♭ Maj over D7
   A min (♭7)
   B7 ♭9 ♯5 13 (1st)

These applications are based on the arbitrary assertion that the root of this scale is B. This scale being symmetrical, you could also call D♯ or G the root.[3] Therefore, the above chords can be transposed up or down a major third and applied to this same scale.

When the augmented scale is broken down into diatonic thirds we get all major third intervals.

When the Augmented scale is broken down into diatonic 4ths, we get: perf. 4th, perf. 5th, perf. 4th, perf. 5th, perf. 4th, perf. 5th.

---

[2] *Enharmonic Spelling*
[3] *see page 10, " There are four of these scales:"*

Note that these "diatonic 4ths" each outline (root-fifth) one of the constituent major (or minor) triads.
EXAMPLE

These Diatonic 4ths sound great when put through the Basic Routine. Because each interval suggests a triad, the effect is one of rapidly shifting tonalities.

The Augmented scale is very effective when used over a static root or repeated bass line because it suggests harmonic motion while staying within the same scale. The Augmented scale is both harmonically and melodically strong.

There are four of these scales:

B+5/C+5 (same as D#+5/E+5, G+5/Ab+5)

C+5/Db+5 (same as E+5/F+5, Ab+5/A+5)

C#+5/D+5 (same as F+5/Gb+5, A+5/Bb+5)

D+5/Eb+5 (same as F#+5/G+5, Bb+5/B+5)

TRITONE SCALE

The Tritone scale is derived from two major triads a tritone apart.
EXAMPLE: C Maj./F# Maj.

It can be used as a substitute for a Diminished scale which, in this case, would be formed by adding the tones E♭ and A to the above Tritone scale.
The related Diminished scale being:

The Tritone scale contains three tritone intervals, whereas the Diminished scale contains four tritone intervals.
Personally, I prefer the Tritone scale to the Diminished scale because it tends to create more of a chordal effect rather than a scale sound. In other terms, more angular, less conjunct. Also, the ♭5-5-♭7-8 sequence gives it a strong Blues sound, while the 1-♭2-3 gives it a somewhat Eastern sound.
Its most obvious applications are:

C7 ♭5 ♭9 (1st)[1]
F# 7 ♭5 ♭9 (Tritone)

And less obvious:

E♭7 ♭9 #9 13 (♭3rd)
A7 ♭9 #9 13 (Maj. 6th)

These four chords are the dominant sevenths that apply to the Diminished scale related to this Tritone scale, as described above. Any other chords over which the related Diminished scale applies, will also work. (i.e.: C#°, E°, F#°, A°)[2]

The Tritone scale sounds good in diatonic 3rds because of the mixture of intervals
EXAMPLE: C/F# TRITONE SCALE IN DIATONIC THIRDS.

I like to use the Tritone scale on tunes where the changes contain dominant 7th chords that last for 2, 4, 8, or more bars and may or may not resolve. (For example, funk tunes, or modal tunes). It's a good contrast from the usual dominant 7th scales. This scale will appear in nearly all chapters of this book.

[1] *See Important Note, page 7.*
[2] *°= Diminished*

CHAPTER 3
TRIAD VARIATIONS

Here are some ways to practice diatonic triads in various scale settings. I'll use C major first to illustrate this. (Do in all keys.)

EXAMPLE: C MAJOR SCALE
First Scheme (for each triad) 3rd, 5th, 3rd, root
  Asc.

  Desc.

Second Scheme (3rd, root, 3rd, 5th)
  Asc.

  Desc.

Now apply this to other diatonic scales: Harmonic Minor, Melodic Minor, Harmonic Major, etc.

Next we apply this to the symmetrical scales: Diminished and Augmented.
EXAMPLE: Diminished scale of C° and D♭°

First Scheme

Asc.

Desc.

Second Scheme

Asc.

Desc.

Don't forget to do all three diminished scales.

EXAMPLE: Augmented scale of B+5 and C+5

First Scheme

Asc.

Desc.

Second Scheme

Asc.

Desc.

Don't forget to do all four Augmented scales.

These two schemes can be applied to pentatonic scales, played in diatonic triads. (Chapter 6 on "Diatonic Intervals and Chords on Scales Containing Fewer than 7 Tones").

EXAMPLE: C Pentatonic; diatonic triads

First Scheme
Asc.

Desc.

Second Scheme
Asc.

Desc.

EXAMPLE: C Pentatonic ♭3, diatonic triads

First Scheme
Asc.

Desc.

Second Scheme
Asc.

Desc.

Also apply these schemes to the Pentatonic ♭6

TRIAD PAIRS

Now we will apply these two schemes to triad pairs. Here we choose two triads to combine (forming a six-note scale). Use two major triads, a tritone apart (tritone scale), two major triads a whole tone apart, one major triad plus one minor triad a whole step below, then two major triads a half step apart.

TWO MAJOR TRIADS, a tritone apart

EXAMPLE: C Maj. plus F♯ Maj.

APPLICATIONS: See Ch. 2, "Tritone Scale"

First Scheme
Asc.

Desc.

Second Scheme
Asc.

Desc.

Do the same with all other Tritone pairs.

TWO MAJOR TRIADS, a whole step apart

EXAMPLE C Maj. and D Maj.

APPLICATIONS:
  C Maj ♯11 or Dom. 7th,♯11
  F♯ 7 ♭9 ♭13 ♭5 (Tritone)*
  E ∅ (3rd)
  D7 sus 11 (2nd)
  A min.7 (Maj. 6th)
  B♭ △ ♯5 (♭7)

See Important Note, page 7

First Scheme
Asc.

Desc.

Second Scheme
Asc.

Desc.

Do the same with all other pairs. Twelve in all.

ONE MAJOR TRIAD AND ONE MINOR TRIAD, a whole step down
EXAMPLE: C Maj. and B♭ Minor

APPLICATIONS:

        C7 ♭9 (1st)
        G7♭5♯9 (Perf. 5)*
        E♭7♭9 (Min. 3rd)
        D♭Maj. 7♯11 (♭2)

First Scheme
Asc.

Desc.

Second Scheme
Asc.

Desc.

Do the same with all other pairs. Twelve in all.

TWO MAJOR TRIADS, one half step apart
EXAMPLE: C Maj. and Db Maj.

APPLICATIONS:

Db Maj./C Maj. (b2)
Db Maj. to C Maj. over Eb7 or
Eb7sus11 to Eb7b9, 13 (b3)
F Harmonic Minor. (Perf. 4th)

18

First Scheme
Asc.

Desc.

Second Scheme
Asc.

Desc.

Do all other pairs. Twelve in all.

I highly recommend exploring all of these scales, not only by playing them through the Basic Routine, but also by playing them through all the other patterns in this book that can be applied (chord/scale, Lower Neighbor Tone, etc).

CHAPTER 4
LOWER NEIGHBOR TONES

Lower Neighbor Tones (1/2 step, symbolized with L.N.T.) leading to lowest member of scale intervals such as diatonic thirds and fourths. *

EXAMPLE: C Major Scale in 3rds w/L.N.T.
    Asc.

    Desc.

EXAMPLE: C Major Scale in 4ths w/L.N.T.
    Asc.

    Desc.

Do in all Major keys.

EXAMPLE: C Harmonic Minor in 3rds w/L.N.T.
    Asc.

    Desc.

---

* See Page 6, "Diatonic 3rds, and "Diatonic 4ths"

C Harmonic Minor in 4ths w/L.N.T.
Asc.

Desc.

Do on all Harmonic Minor Scales.

C Melodic Minor in 3rds w/L.N.T.
Asc.

Desc.

C Melodic Minor in 4ths w/L.N.T.
Asc.

Desc.

Do on all melodic minor scales.

C Auxiliary Diminished Scale in 3rds w/L.N.T.
Asc.

Desc.

C Auxiliary Diminished Scale in 4ths w/L.N.T.
Asc.

Desc.

Do the same with the other two Auxiliary Diminished Scales.

Tritone (C-F♯) scale in 3rds w/L.N.T.
Asc.

Desc.

22

Tritone scale (C-F#) in 4ths w/L.N.T.
Asc.

Desc.

Also do with the other five Tritone scales.

Augmented scale in 3rds with L.N.T. (B+5-C+5)
Asc.

Desc.

Augmented scale in 4ths with L.N.T. (B+5-C+5)
Asc.

Desc.

Apply to other 3 Augmented scales.

C Pentatonic Scale in 3rds w/L.N.T.
   Asc.

   Desc.

C Pentatonic Scales in 4ths w/L.N.T.
   Asc.

   Desc.

Do all twelve Pentatonic Scales.

C Pentatonic ♭6 Scale in 3rds w/L.N.T.
   Asc.

   Desc.

C Pentatonic ♭6 Scale in 4ths w/L.N.T.
Asc.

Desc.

Do on all twelve Pentatonic ♭6 Scales.

C Pentatonic ♭3 Scale in 3rds w/L.N.T.
Asc.

Desc.

C Pentatonic ♭3 Scale in 4ths w/L.N.T.
Asc.

Desc.

Do on all twelve Pentatonic ♭3 Scales.

This procedure of adding a lower neighbor tone to the lower member of a diatonic scale interval (3rd or 4th), can likewise be applied to the diatonic intervals within the Harmonic Major Scale; Byzantine, (Major Scale with ♭2 and ♭6), or any other scale.

Lower Neighbor Tone leading to the highest member of scale intervals (diatonic 3rds and 4ths). **Important:** Scale intervals here are higher note to lower note (inverted order) i.e., 3-1, 4-2, 5-3, etc.

EXAMPLE: C Major Scale in 3rds with lower neighbor tone to higher member of scale interval.

Asc.

Desc.

EXAMPLE: C Major Scale in 4ths with the lower neighbor tone to higher member of interval.

Asc.

Desc.

Do in all keys.

The procedure of adding a lower neighbor note to the higher member of a diatonic scale interval (3rd or 4th)[1], must likewise be applied to the diatonic intervals within the Harmonic Minor Scale, Melodic Minor Scale, Tritone Scale, Augmented Scale, Harmonic Major Scale, Byzantine (Harmonic Major ♭2) Scale, Pentatonic Scale, Pentatonic ♭3 Scale, etc.

If you have trouble hearing any of these or cannot keep them straight in your head while practicing them, try the following: Write out the particular scale you are practicing in diatonic 3rds (or 4ths), then add the lower chromatic neighbor note to the highest note in each interval. Practice that version until it is in your ear and feels somewhat familiar.

EXAMPLE: C Harmonic Minor In 4ths

Again, I must stress the importance of first learning all of the basic diatonic interval patterns before going into the neighbor tone patterns. Failing to do this will make it almost impossible to hear and understand what you are doing, and will usually only confuse you.

---

1. *Important! Remember: In this pattern the scale intervals go from the highest member to the lowest member (i.e. 3-1, 4-2, 5-3, etc.).*

2. *On the following pages, some of the Lower Neighbor Tones are notated like grace notes. This is for visual ease. Play them with equal value to the other notes.*

Now, to extend this system of adding a lower (chromatic) neighbor tone to diatonic scale intervals, we will add one and two more notes to each interval group (or pair). These added note(s) will be of the same diatonic interval distance as the first interval. (i.e., all diatonic 3rd or 4ths). This will form diatonic triads or diatonic 7ths.

Thus, in C Major

So, C Major in diatonic 3rds w/Lower Neighbor Tone (to lower members of each interval)
Asc.

will become C Major in diatonic **triads** w/ Lower Neighbor Tones (to lower member)
Asc.

or, by adding yet another note, becomes C Major, in diatonic 7ths w/ Lower Neighbor Tone to lower member.
Asc.

This procedure is applied to diatonic 4ths, resulting in C Major in diatonic 4ths w/ Lower Neighbor Tone to lowest member,
Asc.

becoming C Major in diatonic 4ths **triads** w/ Lower Neighbor Tone to lowest member.
Asc.

By adding yet another note, it becomes C Major in Diatonic 4ths (4 notes) w/ Lower Neighbor Tone (to lowest member).
Asc.

Appyling the procedure of adding a Lower Neighbor Tone to the highest member of a scale interval and to inverted diatonic triads and 7ths we get:

C Major Diatonic Triads (inverted) w/Lower Neighbor Tone to highest member.

Asc.

Desc.

C Major in Diatonic 7ths (inverted) w/ Lower Neighbor Tone to highest member.

Asc.

Desc.

Likewise we will add the Lower Neighbor Tone to the highest member of groups of diatonic 4ths (inverted) to get C Major in Diatonic 4ths (group of 3) with Lower Neighbor Tone to highest member.

Asc.

Desc.

C Major in diatonic 4ths (group of 4) with Lower Neighbor Tone to the highest member.

Asc.

Desc.

Again, all of these patterns are used not only on major scale, but also on Harmonic Minor, Melodic Minor, Diminished, Tritone, Augmented, Harmonic Major, etc.

Important: Read page 4 of Chapter 1, "How to Practice Patterns" and apply it to this chapter's patterns.

You can invent more patterns yourself after you have mastered the basic ones in this chapter. One suggestion is to simply compound or combine existing patterns. Here are a few suggestions:

In C Major Enhanced Diatonic 7ths

Or

The possibilities are almost endless!

A pattern that is similar to the neighbor tone pattern is as follows:
EXAMPLE: On C Major Diatonic 3rds
　　Asc.

　　Desc.

Experiment with this one!

CHAPTER 5
INTERVAL SETS

Now we will work with a three note unit that outlines a tonality by virtue of the perfect fifth, with added 2nd degree scale step. In other terms, 1, 2, 5 scale degrees or steps.

EXAMPLE: Unit of C

This unit suggests the toniality of C, but is neither major nor minor. It may be considered as either a root postion structure, or an upper structure over another root. Start by playing each unit (all 12) in all inversions.

Example in C:

Asc.

Desc.

Inverted

Asc.

Desc.

Alternating

Asc.

Desc.

Play all units at Expanding Intervals.
Chromatically

Asc.

Desc.

Chromatically, Inverted

Asc.

Desc.

Chromatically, Alternating

Asc.

Desc.

Note: Also start alternating form on C♯, so that each unit will play up and down.

In Whole Steps

Asc.

Desc.

Also start on C♯ (to include other Whole Tone Scale root movement).

In Whole Steps, Inverted

Asc.

Desc.

Also start on G♯ or with C♯ unit.

In Whole Steps, Alternating
   Asc.

  Desc.

Start also on the D unit to reverse unit direction.

Also start on C♯ (to get other Whole Tone Scale), then on D♯ (to reverse order).

In Minor 3rds
   Asc.

  Desc.

Start also on D♭ and D natural.

In Minor Thirds, Inverted
  Asc.

  Desc.

In Minor Thirds, Alternating
  Asc.

  Desc.

Start also on D♭ and D natural.

Do alternating pattern, starting on 2nd group (E♭, if you started with C natural).

In Major 3rds
   Asc.

   Desc.

Start also on C♯, D, E♭, units.

In Major 3rds, Inverted
   Asc.

   Desc.

Start also on C♯, D, E♭, units.

In Major 3rds, Alternating
   Asc.

   Desc.

Start also on C♯, D, E♭.
Do alternating patterns starting on the 2nd unit. (E natural, if you started on C).

Continue preceding patterns at intervals of perfect 4th i.e.

and Tritone.

The distance between each unit (steps 1, 2, 5) can be expanded further if it is practical to do so on your particular instrument.

Now we combine two of these Interval Sets to form various chords. In this combination we play first one unit then the other, alternating. Each unit will appear in two forms: Its root position and its 2nd inversion (starting on its 5th). Accordingly, if we combine, for example, the sets from C and E♭ , we get

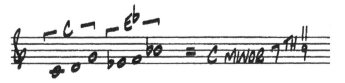

In the sequence described above, it is played

C, in root position

E♭, in root position
C, in 2nd inversion

E♭, in 2nd inversion

Asc.

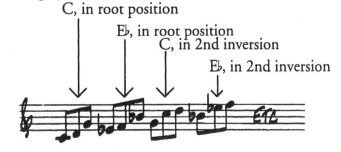

Desc.

IMPORTANT: Notice that each of these units starts on a chord tone of C Minor 7th.

Playing these units in inverted position we get: C-E♭
Asc.

Desc.

Alternating
Asc.

Desc.

The patterns on these last 2 pages should be transposed to all keys (all 12 Minor 7th chords).

---

¹In this alternating unit it is the lowest note (pitch-wise), that is a chord tone of C Minor 7th, not the first note.

Just as we combined the two interval sets whose roots are a Minor 3rd apart, we can combine two units whose roots are a Major 3rd apart.

For example:

in the same sequence described on page 33.

C in root position
E in root position
C in 2nd inversion
E in 2nd inversion

Asc.

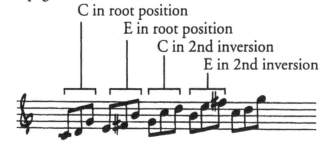

Desc.

IMPORTANT: Notice that each of these units starts on a chord tone of C Major 7th.

Inverted
Asc.

Desc.

Alternating
Asc.

Desc.

These patterns should be transposed to all 12 Major 7 ♯11 chords.

---

[2] *In this alternating unit, it is the lowest note (pitch-wise) that is a chord tone of Major 7th ♯11, not the first note.*

The Minor 7th and Major 7th #11 chords patternized on the preceding pages can be further patternized by extracting a six note spelling of each chord and treating it as follows:

EXAMPLE: C Minor 7th Played as:

is patternized at expanding intervals.

EXAMPLE: Minor 7ths in half steps

Asc.

Desc.

In Whole Steps

Asc.

Desc.

36

Proceed with chords in Minor 3rds, Major 3rds, etc.* Then do all the same using the Major 7th #11, again using the expanding interval routine .

EXAMPLE: Major #11 Chords In Half Steps

Asc.

Desc.

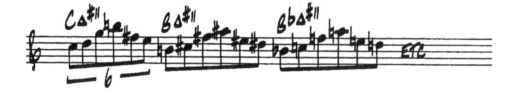

In Whole Steps

Asc.

Desc.

Start also on B △ #11

Proceed with chords in Minor Thirds, Major Thirds, etc.

---

*When continuing the expanding interval routine for the chord sequences on pages 35 and 36, remember: at chord root interval of minor third, start sequence on C, D♭, and D; at Major Third, start on C, D♭, D, E♭.

Now we will consider combining two 1, 2, 5 units a Tritone apart.

Alternate between the C unit and then F♯ unit, putting each unit in the inversion needed to establish the most conjunct possible sequence of alteration.

EXAMPLE: C and F♯

Asc.

Desc.

In reverse order

Asc.

Desc.

Alternating

Asc.

Desc.

The combining of these two units a Tritone apart creates a scale.

EXAMPLE: C and F#

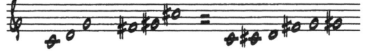

(See Chapter 6 "Diatonic Intervals and Chords from Scales With Fewer than 7 Tones". Also, Chapter 7 "Chord Scale Exercise").

Accordingly the chord-scale exercise can be applied

Asc.

Desc.

Other variations

Or

Or diatonic 3rds (See Chapter 6).

Keep in mind, as I mentioned earlier, many of the forms described in this section should be considered also as upper structures of chords.

EXAMPLE: The CMajor 7#11 formed from

could be considered an upper structure of: A Minor, D9 sus 11, B 7 sus 11 ♭2, etc.

And of course any single 1, 2, 5 unit could be used over one of many roots. You should experiment for yourself to find ones you prefer.

EXAMPLE:

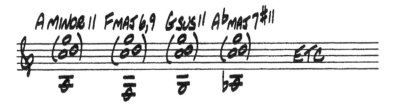

Another interval set (or unit) to consider is one built on 1, ♭3, #5, 7 or Minor 3rd, Perfect 4th, Minor 3rd.

EXAMPLE: From C

Notice that this form contains an A♭ triad with both the Major 3rd (at the bottom) and the Minor 3rd (at the top).

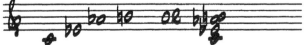

If you refer to the "Scales" chapter, you'll notice that the Diminished and Augmented Scales each contain triads with both Major and Minor 3rds. Accordingly, if this interval set is played in sequence of a Minor 3rd apart, it forms a Diminished Scale. Also, if played a Major 3rd apart, an Augmented Scale is formed.

At a Minor 3rd from C you get:

which form a Diminished Scale.

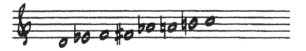

(Start also from D♭ and D natural to get the other Diminished Scales).

At a Major 3rd from C you get:

which forms an Augmented Scale.

(Start also from D♭, D natural, E♭, to get the other Augmented Scales.)

CHAPTER 6
DIATONIC INTERVALS AND CHORDS FROM SCALES CONTAINING FEWER THAN SEVEN TONES

In the case of scales that have fewer than 7 tones, the construction of diatonic chords will require using every other note ascending from each scale step.

(The diatonic 3rds and chords shown in this chapter should be practiced using the "Basic Routine" and the "Triad Variation" Chapters 1 and 3)

For example, the Pentatonic scale has five tones. Determine every other note as follows.

C Pentatonic

The beamed groups illustrate the every other note groupings.

Diatonic 3rds for C Pentatonic are:

Diatonic triads are:

(Note that although these are diatonic triads, not all intervals are generic 3rds). To continue, four note chords on C Pentatonic are likewise built, using every other note.

Likewise we construct diatonic 3rds and chords on the Pentatonic ♭3. Every other note groups are:

C Pentatonic ♭3 in Diatonic 3rds are:

Diatonic triads are:

Diatonic Four Note Chords are:

Likewise construct diatonic 3rds and chords on **Pentatonic ♭6** Scale.

Every other note groups on C Pentatonic ♭6 are:

Diatonic 3rds are:

Diatonic Triads are:

Diatonic Four Note Chords are:

Another scale containing fewer than seven tones is the Augmented Scale which contains six tones. (See Augmented Scale, page 9).

EXAMPLE: The B+5/C+5 Augmented Scale.
The every other note groups are:

At this point please note that because of its symmetrical structure, the 3rds, triads, and four note chords are likewise symmetrical. That is, all the intervals are the same. They are Major 3rds (making Augmented triads). So, diatonic 3rds are:

Diatonic triads are:

Four note chords are:

Another scale containing six notes is the **Tritone Scale** (see page.9). Here we use the same "every other note" procedure to determine diatonic 3rds and chords.

EXAMPLE: C/F♯ Tritone Scale "every other note groups"

Notice how the diatonic 3rds, triads, and four note chords are either contained in, or actually spell out, one or the other of the scale's two constituent chords, C Major or F♯ Major. Thus, Diatonic 3rds are:

Triads

Four Note Chords

For more scales with fewer than seven tones, see pages 15, 16, 17 and 33.

CHAPTER 7
CHORD/SCALE EXERCISE

This pattern incorporates both the stepwise scale form and its constituent diatonic chords. To first grasp this pattern, use it on Major or Minor scales. When applied to other scales such as the Symmetrical scales, Interval Set Pairs, and Pentatonic scales, the form and structure will change somewhat to fit the peculiarities of each scale.

I'll start with C Major to illustrate this, as it should be easy to hear. The pattern consists of (in this case) each diatonic 7th of the scale, alternating with the stepwise scale form.

EXAMPLE: In C Major

Asc.

Desc.

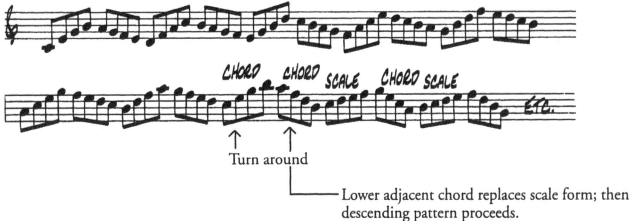

The tricky part of this pattern is the turning around between the ascending form and the descending form. The rule is this: to turn around, instead of following an ascending chord with a descending scale form, follow it with the adjacent descending chord form just below.

EXAMPLE:

Turn around

Lower adjacent chord replaces scale form; then descending pattern proceeds.

It is very important to practice this pattern in all Major keys to make sure you understand it. Then proceed to the Minor keys. Pay special attention to turning around at the top of the pattern.

Here is the Chord/Scale pattern on two Symmetrical scales; the Diminished scale, and the Augmented scale.

EXAMPLE: Chord/Scale Exercise On Diminished Scale of B dim. and C dim.

Asc.

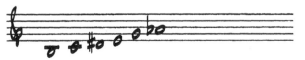

(Also do other Diminished scales).

Chord/scale exercise on Augmented scale. (Refer to Chapter 6 on "Diatonic Intervals and Chords from Scales Containing Fewer than 7 Tones").

EXAMPLE: Scale of B+5/C+5

Asc.

EXAMPLE: C Pentatonic

Asc.

Be sure to do this on Pentonic ♭3 and Pentatonic ♭6. (also see Chapter 5, "Interval Sets").

Chord/scale exercise on "Triad Pair" scales, (See Chapter 6.)
EXAMPLES: C Tri-tone Scale

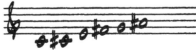

Asc.

EXAMPLE: Triad Pair; Two Major Triads, a Whole Tone Apart.
C Major/D Major

Asc.

(Do all other pairs).

Continue experimenting with any other pairs of triads, including ones discussed in this book, as well as any others you can find that will work. (The two chords making up a pair should have no common tones).

General Chord/Scale Cross Reference Chart
(for Scales discussed in text)*

On any given chord, various scales may be used, depending on the chord's context and harmonic function as well as style and other aesthetic considerations. Therefore, on this chart many choices are indicated. On the dominant seventh chords I have indicated only the highest upper structure tone or alteration. Check each reference in the text to determine any other altered tones, and choose accordingly. (For instance, C7 ♯11 may have a 9th or a ♭9th). The text will indicate transposition needed to determine which chords fit a particular scale.

On this chart, the numbers in the boxes indicate the chord tone from which each particular scale starts (is rooted). For instance, using the chart to find a scale on A ⌀ (half diminished), look in the boxes after "Half Diminished". In the Pentatonic ♭3 column you see the chord tone number ♭3. This means that on A ⌀ the appropriate Pentatonic ♭3 scale starts (is rooted) on the flat three.

Note: No chart or list is entirely complete. Explore on your own!

Scales

	Pentatonic	Pentatonic ♭3	Pentatonic ♭6	Augmented	Tritone	Triad Pair. Two Major Triads at W.T.	Triad Pair. Two Major Triads at 1/2 Step	Triad Pair. One Major and One Minor at W.T.	See Chapter 5
Major 7th	1 5			7					
Major 7th ♯11	1 2 5	6	3			1		page 16	page 34
Major 7th ♯5	2	6	1 3	7		2			
Minor 7th	♭3	1		2		♭3			page 33
Minor △		1	5	2					
Half Diminished		♭3	♭7			♭6			
Dominant 7th ♯5		♭2	1 ♯5	1					
Dominant 7th ♭9		♭2	♯5	1 ♭2	1, ♭3 ♭5, 6	♭5	6	page 16	
Dominant 7th ♯9		♭2	♯5		1, ♭3 ♭5, 6	♭5		page 16	
Dominant 7th 11(sus4)	1, 4, 6, 7	5		♭2		♭7			page 38-9
Dominant 7th ♯11		5	2	♭2	1	1			
Dominant 7th ♭13		4	1			♭5			
Dominant 7th sus 11 ♭2		♭7	4	1					

* *Clarification of Terms, page 6.*